# SECRET SACRED SITES

*Martin Gray*

JONGLEZ PUBLISHING

For Mark Schultz who has given me twenty years of extraordinary assistance
in creating my World Pilgrimage Guide at sacredsites.com

Malekallu Tirupathi Hilltop Temple – Karnataka, Arasikere – India

# Introduction

In 2004 the North American publisher Barnes & Noble published my book, *Sacred Earth: Places of Peace and Power*. The book had beautiful colour photographs of 150 of the world's most iconic and well-known pilgrimage places. The Introduction, which may be read on my website World Pilgrimage Guide at sacredsites.com, discusses the location of sacred sites and how we may explain their powers and their effect on visitors. I recommend you take a few moments to read that Introduction because it will give you an understanding of the places shown in this current book, *Secret Sacred Sites*.

The sites in this book are little known outside the regions where they are located and the religions practised at them. Some are visited by large numbers of pilgrims every year, others by far smaller numbers. A few are listed in travel guidebooks, while most will only be known to cultural anthropologists and the pilgrims who visit them.

In 1982 I had a series of remarkable visionary experiences that initiated my travels to these sacred sites. During the following four decades, I travelled extensively, visiting, studying and photographing more than 2,000 pilgrimage sites in 160 countries. Along the way, I read much about archaeology, religion, mythology and shamanism. Many of these scholarly sources are noted in the references on the World Pilgrimage Guide website. I also continued to have visionary experiences at different sacred sites. These experiences, along with my studies, gave me year by year a deeper understanding of sacred sites and the importance and benefits of visiting them.

I learned that there are three broad categories of visitors to the sacred sites. By far the largest number are traditional pilgrims: Buddhists, Christians, Hindus and Muslims going to their respective religions' holy places. In the second category are tourists visiting places of monumental architecture in various countries – Stonehenge in England, the Great Pyramids in Egypt, Machu Picchu in Peru – that had been sacred sites long before the development of tourism. And third, an increasing number of people like myself are drawn to these places for reasons other than religion or tourism. Over four decades, I questioned hundreds of people in this third category and repeatedly heard similar stories about why they had gone to sacred sites.

Some people told me of visions they had experienced since their youth that had compelled them to undertake journeys to these sites. Some mentioned reoccurring dreams about particular holy places that sparked their desire to visit them. Still others spoke of repeatedly seeing photographs of specific sites in magazines and documentaries, almost as if they were being invited by the places to visit them. I heard musings about a mysterious spiritual magnetism exerted by the sacred sites. And occasionally among these explanations, I heard reports of miraculous things that some people had experienced at different sacred sites.

These reports of spiritual magnetism and miraculous experiences did not surprise me because they were an integral part of my own journey. And as I was to learn from studying historical accounts of other pilgrims' journeys and the founding legends of different sacred sites, various types of miracles were often mentioned. While most contemporary scientists will assert that such things are impossible, it is noteworthy that the 4th-century Christian theologian St Augustine (354–430) once said, 'Miracles are not contrary to nature, but only contrary to what we know of nature.'

How might we account for such seemingly miraculous things – a wide variety of which have occurred at sacred sites worldwide since long before the dawn of the historical era? And I emphasise before the start of the historical period because many of the reported miracles come down to us via legends and myths that speak of times preceding the advent of historical writings.

Based on my studies and personal experiences, I suggest several influences that may give rise to the miraculous phenomena reported at different sacred sites. These would be the influences of celestial bodies (which are studied by the science of archaeoastronomy), the influences of different Earth energies, the influences of particular mathematics used in the design and construction of different types of architecture found at the sacred sites, the influences of the stone materials used in the sacred structures, the influences of light and sound, and the power of human intention (as manifested through the intentions of the designers, builders, priests and pilgrims at the sites). I give a detailed examination and discussion of each of these influences on my World Pilgrimage Guide website, which I encourage you to read. Here in this short Introduction, I will bring brief attention to them.

Astrologers assert that different celestial bodies – the Sun, Moon, planets and stars – exert a psychological and physical influence upon people at different places and times. Such claims have been made for thousands of years in a wide variety of cultures around the world. How can we explain them? The force of gravity, still a mystery to science, may give us a hint. It seems that the positional relationship between our planet and other celestial objects may give rise to profound experiences for human beings.

Furthermore, because the celestial bodies have different movement cycles, we may discern repeating patterns of influence marked by specific periods in our calendars. Well-known periods are the solstices, equinoxes, lunar standstills and the horizon appearances of various planets. Several ancient cultures precisely monitored each of these events, which recur with extraordinary frequency in the myths and legends of these cultures. Rather than disregarding these mythic remembrances as the pre-literate imaginations of prehistoric people, I suggest that we bring deeper attention to them and thereby possibly discern something previously unknown or misunderstood.

And what of the so-called 'Earth energies'? We may expand our thinking regarding these by mentioning known energies such as magnetism, electromagnetism, the localised influences of highly concentrated minerals and the presence of flowing underground waters. While such energies may not, for most people, be directly palpable, this does not mean they do not exist. As we may discern the existence of subtle breezes by the observation of

Sankassa – Uttar Pradesh – India

Shirdi Sai Baba Samadhi Mandir – Shirdi, Maharashtra – India

trees moving in the wind on a distant hill, so also may certain sensitive people discern the effects of the known Earth energies by the use of dowsing skills. Such skills have been developed and utilised for thousands of years. It is important to mention that these dowsing tools do not actually locate Earth energies, but instead magnify the response of the human nervous system to those energies.

Ancient legends and historical accounts – including those of Chinese Feng Shui, Hindu Vastu, pre-Columbian Mesoamerica and early Christian Europe – often mention terrestrial lines of power and specific places along those lines where forces, or spirits, are more highly concentrated and available for human use. As confirmation, we should note the remarkable linear arrangement of particular sacred sites over large distances, sometimes called ley lines, and the non-celestially oriented positioning of some temples and early churches. These subjects need further study, which will require a jettisoning of preconceived notions on the researcher's part.

Next, we must consider the mathematics used to design and build sacred structures. Readers may have heard of such terms as the golden ratio, the Fibonacci sequence and sacred geometry. These are particular mathematics used by ancient builders to design and construct megaliths, pyramids, temples, churches and mosques. Similar to the way in which musical instruments such as pianos, flutes and guitars are built with attention to precise mathematical formulas, certain religious structures were also designed and constructed so that the spiritual 'notes' would correctly resonate within them.

The types of stone used in a building were also of importance to ancient builders. This is evident from the frequent use of high-content quartz and magnetic-field rocks such as are found in (and often laboriously transported to) pyramids, megalithic structures and medieval-era European cathedrals. As today's complex computer circuitry depends upon the inclusion of specific minerals, so also were particular mineral types used in the manufacture of different kinds of sacred structures.

Two other important matters when considering the remarkable phenomena reported at sacred sites are the skilful use of light and sound within built holy spaces. The vast, soaring medieval cathedrals dazzle pilgrims with their exquisite stained-glass windows and brilliantly coloured beams of light. Sacred music played on organs echoes throughout the great spaces. Monks and pilgrims – Christian, Hindu, Buddhist and Sufi – chant trance-inducing harmonies accompanied by drums, bells and wind instruments. The poet Goethe once said that sacred architecture is frozen music. And within such architecture, the sacredness is amplified by glorious sights and sounds. Visiting sacred sites today brings you into these realms.

We should also note the question of human intention and its profound influence on people's experiences within the different sacred spaces. Everyone involved in creating, constructing, managing and using sacred sites contributes to what we might call the field or presence of a holy place. There is a density of holiness that saturates and surrounds the immediate vicinity of pilgrimage sites, and this field of holiness results from the cumulative intentions of all the individuals who have participated in the development and use of the sites over time.

What is the character, quality and nature of this holiness field at the sacred sites? I wondered about this for the first two decades of my visits to pilgrimage places worldwide. I saw men and women, young and old, from various religions expressing what appeared to be a multitude of different emotions. I saw joy and anguish, hope and desperation on pilgrims' faces. I wondered whether there were any common denominators in what I was observing. I found that there were. There were two essential commonalities to what pilgrims were doing. They were saying 'Please' and 'Thank you'. They were praying and expressing gratitude for prayers that had been answered. These intense emotions of the heart and mind preceded and transcended all the different religions practised at the various sacred sites. What I was observing – and feeling myself – was the universality of the yearning and gratitude of the human soul.

Concurrent with this sublime realisation about the power of sacred places and the nature of their sacredness was an understanding of how to personally access it. Ultimately this is very simple and available to anyone, regardless of their religious persuasion or lack thereof. Nothing is required other than simply being present at a sacred site. No beliefs, rituals, priestly assistance or knowledge of religious texts. Only the simple action of being there with an open heart and mind.

You may ask how there could be a transmission of the transformative powers of the sacred sites to a visitor. This is also simple, and an analogy is helpful in explaining it. Consider what happens when a tea bag is put in a cup of hot water: the essence of the tea steeps into the water and imparts its taste. Or what happens when photographic film is exposed to light for a fraction of a second: the light exposes the film, creating an impression of a scene. Or, even more telling, what happens when a computer downloads a file wirelessly: there is a rapid transfer of information from source to receiver.

In addition to what we might call the spiritual essence available at the sacred sites – those distillations of the cumulative expressions of the prayers and gratitude of millions of pilgrims over time – there are also particular energies or powers specific to individual sacred sites.

Ancient legends and modern-day reports tell of extraordinary experiences that people have had while visiting sacred sites. According to these stories, different sacred sites can heal the body, enlighten the mind, increase creativity, develop psychic abilities and awaken the soul to a realisation of its true purpose in life. How can this be explained?

Once again, an analogy is helpful. Consider the human body from an oriental medicine perspective, which states that numerous acupuncture lines or meridians flow throughout the body, each corresponding to a particular organ or system. Likewise, with the Earth, there are planet-spanning lines of force, and places along these lines, that contain and emanate different energetic characteristics. These telluric currents, termed 'lung mei' lines in Chinese Feng Shui, are little known, understood or studied by contemporary science. However, an emerging ethos of spiritual ecology is sponsoring an interest and exploration of the subject.

Tinos pilgrim – Greece

Shirdi Sai Baba Samadhi Mandir – Shirdi, Maharashtra – India

A fascinating related issue is the remarkable correlation between the personality characteristics of different deities venerated at sacred sites and the various energetic qualities of the places. How may we explain this? First, it is noteworthy that some sacred sites are dedicated to masculine or feminine deities. Perhaps this is sometimes an indication of the energetic polarity of the sites or, as Feng Shui practitioners would say, the Yin and Yang essence of the sites.

In addition to this basic positive/negative, masculine/feminine categorisation, there is a wide variety of deities and stories about those deities found in some religions, particularly Hinduism. Here is an important question: did all these different deities exist and perform different actions at different sacred sites or are they better understood as metaphors, as symbols indicating the variety of sacred sites, their different energies and their effects upon people? Based on my studies of religion, mythology and hundreds of sacred site legends, I feel confident in suggesting a connection between the specific energy of particular places, the character of their associated myths and people's experiences at these sites. The myths and legends about sacred places often give insights into how those places will affect you as a visitor.

In closing, I would like to make a few suggestions about using this book and interacting with the sacred sites when you are there. Consider the images in this book, and on the World Pilgrimage Guide website, as *windows to look through* rather than photographs to look at. Additionally, consider that these 'windows' allow for the transfer of the visual homeopathic essence of the sacred sites to you.

You may also use this book and the website as an oracle to determine which sacred sites would benefit you to visit. With this question in mind – what specific sacred site would be good for you to visit? – close your eyes and slowly thumb through the pages. Let the spiritual magnetism of a site or sites reach across space and guide you as to when to stop and open your eyes. There is a remarkable magic to this process. Let the sacred sites choose you rather than the other way around.

When you visit a sacred site, it is important to understand that the energies go both ways. The sacred site affects you, and you also affect the site. A human being may function as an acupuncture needle in the living earth and our spiritual energies can benefit the planet. On the World Pilgrimage Guide website, I explain a simple meditation technique that you can use to consciously focus and direct healing energy into the earth at the sacred sites.

Finally, I would like to briefly discuss the future use of the world's sacred sites. We are entering a Gaian Age of Pilgrimage and there is a paradigm shift in understanding regarding the implications and potency of pilgrimage. A widespread socio-cultural phenomenon is occurring – the awakening and vitalisation of global eco-spiritual consciousness. A transformative spiritual energy is available to human beings, concentrated at specific places across the planet, which catalyses and increases this eco-spiritual consciousness. These places are the sacred sites illustrated in this book and on my World Pilgrimage Guide website. As each of us awakens to a fuller knowledge of our spiritual consciousness, we further empower the global field of eco-spiritual consciousness. That is the deeper meaning and purpose of these magical holy places: they are source points of the power of spiritual illumination.

# Contents


*White Sands,* **New Mexico • USA** .... 20
*Chaco Canyon,* **New Mexico • USA** .... 21
*Nuestra Señora de Luján,* **Luján • Argentina** .... 22
*Sanctuary of Bom Jesus da Lapa,* **Bom Jesus da Lapa • Brazil** .... 23
*Sanctuary of Padre Cícero,* **Brazil** .... 24
*El Infiernito,* **Villa de Leyva • Colombia** .... 26
*Basilica of our Lady of Charity,* **El Cobre • Cuba** .... 27
*Basilica of the Virgin of Socavon,* **Oruro • Bolivia** .... 28
*Church of Our Lady of Candelaria,* **Tlacotalpan • Mexico** .... 29
*Shrine of the Cross of Chalpon,* **Motupe • Peru** .... 30
*Qoyllur Rit'i,* **Sinakara Valley • Peru** .... 31
*Anundshög stones,* **Västerås • Sweden** .... 32
*Sanctuary of Mary,* **La Salette • France** .... 33
*Shrine of Our Lady of Walsingham,* **Walsingham • UK** .... 34
*St David's Cathedral,* **Western Wales • UK** .... 36
*St Nonna's Church,* **Alternun • UK** .... 37
*Shrine of Our Lady of Altötting,* **Germany** .... 38
*Church of Maria Alm,* **Austria** .... 40
*Sanctuary of Madonna del Sasso,* **Locarno • Switzerland** .... 41
*Church of Santa Rosalia,* **Monte Pellegrino, Sicily • Italy** .... 42
*S'Ena'e Thomes,* **Dorgali, Sardinia • Italy** .... 43
*Pecherska Monastery,* **Kiev • Ukraine** .... 44
*Monastery of Pochayiv,* **Pochayiv • Ukraine** .... 45
*Voronet Monastery,* **Voronet • Romania** .... 46
*Tekke of Sari Salltiku,* **Mali i Krujës • Albania** .... 48
*Shrine of Abu Zamaa al-Balawi,* **Kairouan • Tunisia** .... 50
*Mount Oldonyo Lengai,* **Tanzania** .... 51
*Great Zimbabwe,* **Zimbabwe** .... 52
*Maqam Sidi Ahmed al-Badawi,* **Tanta • Egypt** .... 54
*Church of the Virgin Mary,* **Zeitoun • Egypt** .... 55
*Shrine of the Abdurrahman Gazi Mezarligi,* **Erzurum • Turkey** .... 56

*Shrine of Somuncu Baba,* **Darende • Turkey** ..... 57
*Tomb of Rabbi Isaac Luria,* **Safed • Israel** ..... 58
*Shrine of the Bab,* **Haifa • Israel** ..... 59
*Franciscan Church of the Transfiguration,* **Mount Tabor • Israel** ..... 60
*Church of the Assumption,* **Jerusalem • Israel** ..... 62
*Mausoleum of Hasan al-Basri,* **Basra • Iraq** ..... 63
*Mausoleums of Imam Ali Alhadi and Imam Hasan Alaskari,* **Samarra • Iraq** ..... 64
*Mausoleum of Seventh Imam Musa al-Kadhim and Ninth Imam Muhammad al-Jawad,* **Kadhimiya, Baghdad • Iraq** ..... 66
*Mausoleum of al-Sharif al-Radhi,* **Kadhimiya, Baghdad • Iraq** ..... 67
*Mausoleum of Abdul Qadir Gilani,* **Baghdad • Iraq** ..... 68
*The Mausoleum of Alqasim,* **Babylon • Iraq** ..... 69
*Shrines of Muslim ibn Aqeel and Hani ibn Urwa,* **Kufa • Iraq** ..... 70
*Mausoleum of Imam Hussain,* **Karbala • Iraq** ..... 72
*Mausoleum of Abbas,* **Karbala • Iraq** ..... 73
*Shrines of Zoroastrianism,* **Chak Chak • Iran** ..... 74
*Shrine of the Sufi saint Shah Nur-ed-Din Neatollah Vali,* **Mahan • Iran** ..... 76
*Shrine of Imamzade Shah-e' Abdal-Azim,* **Rey • Iran** ..... 77
*Mosque of Jam Karan,* **Jam Karan • Iran** ..... 78
*Mir Movsum Aga Mausoleum,* **Baku • Azerbaijan** ..... 80
*Temple of Garni,* **Armenia** ..... 81
*Sulaiman Too,* **Osh • Kyrgyzstan** ..... 82
*Mausoleum of Ismamut Ata,* **Rey • Iran** ..... 84
*Ak Ishan,* **Ak Ishan • Iran** ..... 85
*Shrine of Baha al-Din al-Naqshbandi,* **Bukhara • Uzbekistan** ..... 86
*Mausoleum of Khoja Ahmed Yasawi,* **Turkestan • Kazakhstan** ..... 87
*Blue Mosque,* **Mazar-e-Sharif • Afghanistan** ..... 88
*Mausoleum of Shah Rukn-e-Alam,* **Multan • Pakistan** ..... 92
*Mausoleum of Hazrat Bahauddin Zakariya,* **Multan • Pakistan** ..... 93
*Varasidhi Vinayaka Swamy Temple,* **Kanipakam, Andhra Pradesh • India** ..... 94
*Veerabhadra Swamy Temple,* **Lepakshi, Andhra Pradesh • India** ..... 95
*Sivadol Temple,* **Sivasagar, Assam • India** ..... 96
*Surya Pahar,* **Assam • India** ..... 100
*Tilinga Mandir,* **Bordubi, Assam • India** ..... 104

*Mandar Hill,* **Bihar • India** ... 106
*Mundeshwari Devi Temple,* **Bihar • India** ... 106
*Maa Bamleshwari Temple,* **Chhattisgarh • India** ... 110
*Chamunda Devi Temple,* **Himachal Pradesh • India** ... 112
*Renuka Temple,* **Himachal Pradesh • India** ... 114
*Baba Garib Nath Temple,* **Himachal Pradesh • India** ... 118
*Mahaganapati Temple,* **Gokarna, Karnataka • India** ... 120
*Talakaveri Temple,* **Karnataka • India** ... 121
*Mahaganapathi Temple,* **Madhur, Kerala • India** ... 122
*Guruvayur Krishna Temple,* **Kerala • India** ... 124
*Sabarimala Temple,* **Kerala • India** ... 125
*Khandoba Marthanda Bhairava Temple,* **Jejuri, Maharashtra • India** ... 126
*Tulja Bhavani Mandir,* **Tuljapur, Maharashtra • India** ... 128
*Ramkund,* **Nashik, Maharashtra • India** ... 130
*Great Stupa,* **Sanchi, Madhya Pradesh • India** ... 132
*Huma Leaning Temple,* **Odisha • India** ... 133
*Siddha Jagannath Temple,* **Odisha • India** ... 134
*Maa Tara Tarini Temple,* **Purushottampour, Odisha • India** ... 135
*Willong Khullen,* **Manipur • India** ... 136
*Kapil Muni Temple,* **West Bengal • India** ... 138
*Shiva Natraja Temple,* **Chidambaram, Tamil Nadu • India** ... 142
*Arulmigu Patteswar Swamy Temple,* **Coimbatore, Tamil Nadu • India** ... 143
*Saranatha Perumal Vishnu Temple,* **Tirucherai, Tamil Nadu • India** ... 144
*Sri Jogulamba Ammavari Temple,* **Alampur, Telangana • India** ... 146
*Gorakhnath Temple,* **Gorakhpur, Uttar Pradesh • India** ... 148
*Chakra Tirtha,* **Naimisharanya, Uttar Pradesh • India** ... 149
*Tomb and Shrine of Kabir,* **Magahar, Uttar Pradesh • India** ... 150
*Hanuman Garhi Temple,* **Naimisharanya, Uttar Pradesh • India** ... 151
*Mahaparinirvana Stupa,* **Kushinagar, Uttar Pradesh • India** ... 152
*Kedarnath Temple,* **Uttarakhand • India** ... 154
*Makhdoom Sahib Dargah,* **Srinagar, Kashmir • India** ... 155
*Amarnath Temple,* **Kashmir • India** ... 156
*Nagadeepa Purana Rajamaha Viharaya,* **Nainathevu island • Sri Lanka** ... 158
*Muktinath Temple,* **Nepal** ... 159

*Janakpuri Temple,* **Janakpur • Nepal** ..... 160
*Budanilkantha,* **Kathmandu • Nepal** ..... 161
*Chimi Lhakhang Temple,* **Punakha district • Bhutan** ..... 162
*Monastery of Tharpaling,* **Bhutan** ..... 163
*Buli Goempa Monastery,* **Bhutan** ..... 164
*Kurjey Lhakhang,* **Bumthang • Bhutan** ..... 166
*Demchig Hiid Monastery,* **Mongolia** ..... 168
*Tuvkhun Monastery,* **Shireet Ulaan Uul • Mongolia** ..... 169
*Han Bogd Hairham,* **Mongolia** ..... 170
*Galvan Zuu Temple,* **Tsetserleg • Mongolia** ..... 172
*Monastery of Toling,* **Tibet** ..... 173
*Puji Si Temple,* **Pu Tuo Shan • China** ..... 174
*Saoba Stone Pillars,* **Ruisui • Taiwan** ..... 175
*Chaotian Temple,* **Beigang • Taiwan** ..... 176
*Fo Guang Shan Temple,* **Kaohsiung • Taiwan** ..... 177
*Cave Temple of Sanbangsa,* **Jeju Island • South Korea** ..... 178
*Hwaeomsa Monastery,* **Mount Jirisan • South Korea** ..... 179
*Taebaek-san,* **South Korea** ..... 180
*Chùa Bà Thiên Hâu Pagoda,* **Saigon • Vietnam** ..... 181
*Thien Mu Pagoda,* **Hue • Vietnam** ..... 182
*Koh Ker,* **Cambodia** ..... 183
*Wat Phabat Phonsane,* **Phabath • Laos** ..... 184
*That Sikhottabong Stupa,* **Thakhek • Laos** ..... 185
*Shwe Mawdaw Pagoda,* **Bago • Myanmar** ..... 186
*Candi Sukuh,* **Mount Lawu • Java, Indonesia** ..... 188
*Lore Lindu National Park,* **Besoa, Bada, Napu • Sulawesi, Indonesia** ..... 190
*Batu Caves Temple,* **Kuala Lumpur • Malaysia** ..... 194
*Ishibutai Kofun,* **Asuka • Japan** ..... 196
*Ishi no Hoden,* **Takasago • Japan** ..... 198
*Shinto Shrine of Futami Okitama,* **Ise • Japan** ..... 200
*San Agustin Church,* **Paoay, Luzon • Philippines** ..... 201
*Mount Wollumbin,* **Australia** ..... 202

# *White Sands*

## **New Mexico • USA**

In south-central New Mexico, USA, are the world's largest dune fields of gypsum sand. The brilliant white dunes cover an area of nearly 230 square miles, with many dunes rising to over 60 feet. The dunes were a fabled site for vision-quests of Indians throughout the southwestern United States and northern Mexico. The dunes also attract visitors from very far away. While National Park and government officials will resolutely deny their existence, hundreds of UFOs have been observed at White Sands during the past 50 years.

# *Chaco Canyon*

## **New Mexico • USA**

Deep in the remote deserts of north-western New Mexico, USA, lie the extensive ruins of the most outstanding architectural achievement of the North American Indians known as the Anasazi. Called the Chaco Canyon complex and existing from 700 to 1150, when drought caused it to be abandoned, the site was the main social and ceremonial centre of the Anasazi culture.

# *Nuestra Señora de Luján*

## Luján • Argentina

Sixty-eight kilometres west of Buenos Aires, the capital of Argentina, stands the city of Luján, famous for its great basilica dedicated to Mary, Our Lady of Luján (Nuestra Señora de Luján). Construction began in 1887 and was completed in 1935. Our Lady of Luján is the patron saint of Argentina, Paraguay and Uruguay. Approximately 6 million people visit the shrine annually, many coming during the four significant pilgrimage periods. The feast days of Nuestra Señora de Luján are celebrated on 8 May and 8 December.

# *Sanctuary of Bom Jesus da Lapa*

## Bom Jesus da Lapa • Brazil

The Sanctuary of Bom Jesus da Lapa in Brazil is a natural limestone cave discovered by the Portuguese priest Francisco Mendonça Mar in 1691. The cave church is home to the third-largest Catholic festival in Brazil, attracting as many as 800,000 visitors annually. The annual pilgrimage, Romaria do Bom Jesus da Lapa, takes place from July 18 to August 6, and celebrates the site's mythological importance in Brazilian Catholicism.

# *Sanctuary of Padre Cícero*

## **Brazil**

Nestled in the heart of north-eastern Brazil, the sanctuary of Padre Cícero was constructed in honour of Father Cícero Romão Batista in the late 19th century. Padre Cícero (1844–1934), who was ordained as a priest in 1870, was renowned as a miraculous healer with supernatural powers. He preached a theology focused on social justice and advocated for agrarian reform. In 1889 he founded a religious city called Juazeiro do Norte, which became a major pilgrimage site and the base of his ministry. Each November (the priest's birth month) sees an upsurge of devout pilgrims flocking to the sanctuary.

AVISO

# *El Infiernito*

## Villa de Leyva • Colombia

Located 8 km to the west of the colonial-era town of Villa de Leyva, the ruins of El Infiernito ('The Little Hell') are one of Colombia's most unusual ancient sites. The site has several notable features, including two lines of 36 standing stones with distinct solar and astronomical orientations and 30 tall stone columns with definite phallic shapes, which archaeologists suggest were used in fertility rituals. Archaeological investigations indicate that the site was used for ceremonial purposes as long ago as 2000 BCE, and it was an important holy place of the Muisca Indians from 1000 to 1550 CE.

# *Basilica of our Lady of Charity*

## El Cobre • Cuba

There are two pilgrimage shrines in Cuba, the Basilica of Our Lady of Charity in El Cobre, near Santiago in the eastern part of the island, and the Church of San Lázaro, near Havana in the west. The much-venerated statue of the Virgin Mary at El Cobre was discovered by two fishermen in the 17th century. The present basilica, completed in 1926, houses the cherished icon. Pilgrims visit El Cobre throughout the year, with a peak during the annual Feast of Our Lady of Charity on 8 September. In Cuba, the Virgin of Charity is also much favoured by the followers of Santería, a syncretic religion of West African and Caribbean origin. The Virgin is synonymous with Oshun, the Santería orisha (saint) of love and dancing.

# *Basilica of the Virgin of Socavon*

## **Oruro • Bolivia**

The Basilica of the Virgin of Socavon in Oruro, Bolivia, contains a miraculous image of the Virgin Mary that appeared in 1781. Known as the Virgin of the Mineshaft, she is the patron saint of miners. The exciting Oruro Carnival each February culminates in a grand procession to her sanctuary. On the hill overlooking the town and basilica is a 45-metre-high statue of the Virgin of Socavon, which is 7 metres higher than the statue of Christ in Rio de Janeiro, Brazil.

# *Church of Our Lady of Candelaria*

## **Tlacotalpan • Mexico**

Tlacotalpan, Mexico, is home to the beautiful Church of Our Lady of Candelaria, which honours the appearance of the Virgin Mary. Pilgrimages to the church have been taking place since the 18th century. The annual Feast of Candelaria in February draws large numbers of pilgrims, who enjoy a week of festivities, with musical performances and hundreds of stalls selling delicious local foods. On 2 February the miraculous statue of Mary is taken for a boat ride on the Papaloapan River.

# *Shrine of the Cross of Chalpon*

## **Motupe • Peru**

The small town of Motupe, in the Lambayeque region of Peru, is famous for its cave shrine of the Cross of Chalpon. The cave, once the home of a hermit priest named Padre Juan, hosts a miraculous wooden cross discovered on Mount Chalpon. The revered cross has been an object of devotion since the early 19th century. Each year on 5 August, there is a pilgrimage festival in which devotees carry the Cross of Chalpon from the cave to the village of Motupe. Many of the pilgrims attending the festival walk barefoot from all over Peru.

# *Qoyllur Rit'i*

## Sinakara Valley • Peru

Qoyllur Rit'i is a syncretic religious festival held annually at the Sinakara Valley in the southern highlands of Peru. The annual three-day Qoyllur Rit'i festival in May or June celebrates the reappearance of the Pleiades constellation in the sky. Events include processions of holy icons and dances in and around the Shrine of the Lord of Qoyllur Rit'i. The festival has been celebrated for thousands of years and is attended by more than 100,000 pilgrims every year.

# *Anundshög stones*

## **Västerås • Sweden**

Sweden's Anundshög stone ring whispers ancient tales of a time long past. This sacred site, dating back to the Iron Age, consists of large standing stones arranged in a striking ship-like formation. It is believed to be related to the worship of the Norse god Freyr. The stone ring, which is probably 1,000 years old, has been a place of pilgrimage and celebration since its creation. Midsummer and other pagan festivals are celebrated at Anundshög, emphasising its enduring mythological significance.

# *Sanctuary of Mary*

## La Salette • France

Nestled amidst the French Alps, the Sanctuary of Mary in La Salette, France, is a revered site of Marian apparitions. This holy place commemorates the 1846 appearance of the Virgin Mary to two shepherd children. The main religious structure, the Basilica of Our Lady of La Salette, was completed in 1864. Pilgrimages peak during the anniversary of the apparition on 19 September and the site's mythological importance continues to inspire devotion from believers.

# *Shrine of Our Lady of Walsingham*

## **Walsingham • UK**

In the heart of England lies the Shrine of Our Lady of Walsingham, a significant place of Marian pilgrimage since the 11th century. The shrine's replica of the Holy House (believed to be where the Annunciation occurred) is particularly noteworthy. By the time of its destruction in 1538, during the reign of Henry VIII, the shrine had become one of the greatest religious centres in England and Europe, together with Glastonbury and Canterbury. After nearly four hundred years, the 20th century saw the restoration of pilgrimages to Walsingham.

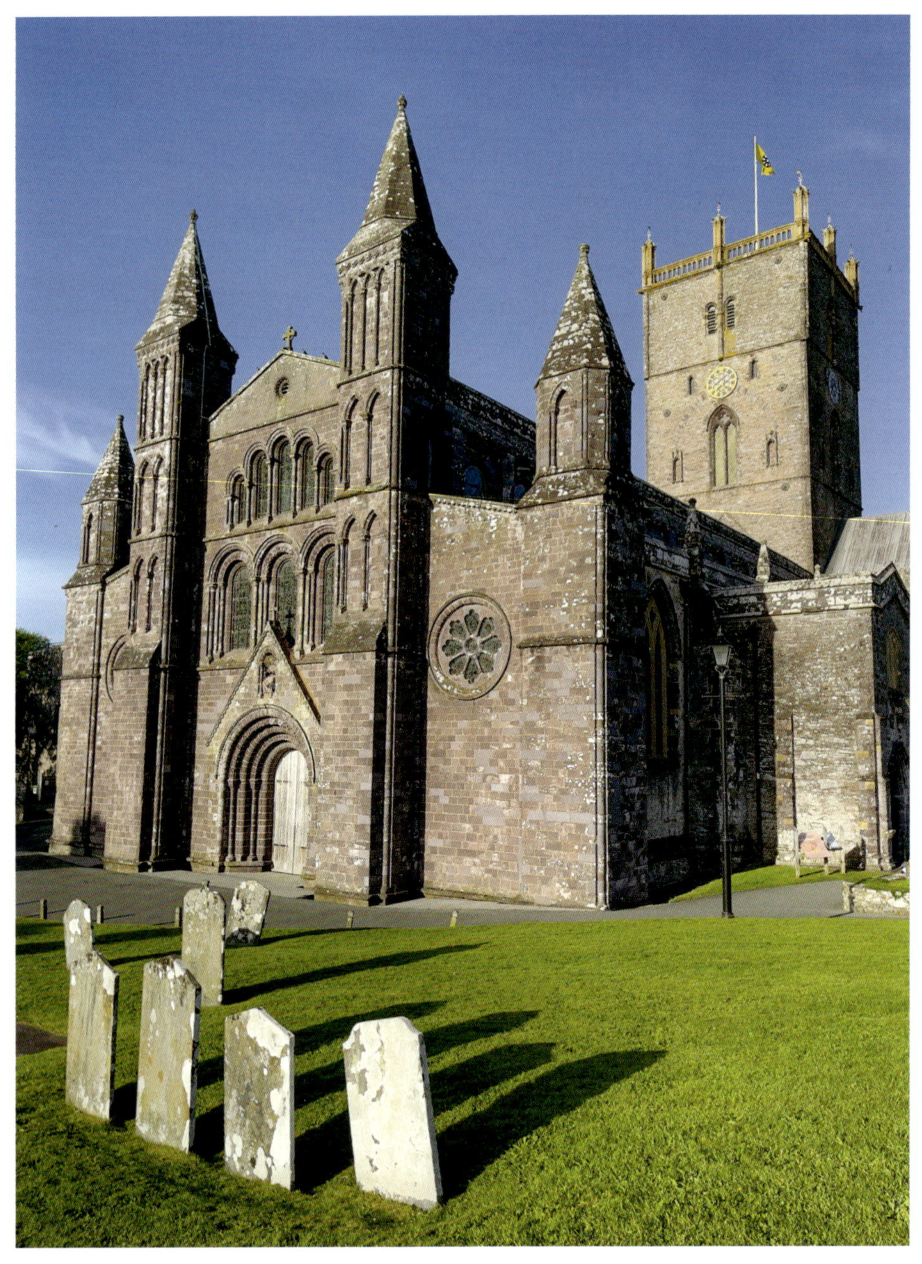

# *St David's Cathedral*

## **Western Wales • UK**

In western Wales, UK, stands St David's Cathedral, a venerated site dedicated to the country's patron saint, St David. Founded in the 6th century, the cathedral has stood since the 12th century, surviving Viking invasions and the ebb and flow of time. Its unique sloping floor and magnificent wooden ceiling are noteworthy architectural elements. Pilgrimages peak on 1 March, St David's Day, with visitors immersing themselves in prayer, reflection and the site's rich history.

# *St Nonna's Church*

## **Alternun • UK**

Standing gracefully in Alternun, Cornwall, UK, is St Nonna's Church. The Normans built a church here in the 12th century but the present granite building dates from the 15th century. The church is dedicated to St Nonna, mother of St David, and is famous for the 79 remarkable wooden bench-ends on the pews dating from between 1510 and 1530. One of Cornwall's finest Norman fonts can be found in the church. This 12th-century square font was originally painted and some paint still clings to the large carvings of bearded faces on each corner.

# *Shrine of Our Lady of Altötting*

## **Germany**

The Shrine of Our Lady of Altötting in Bavaria is one of Germany's most important Catholic pilgrimage sites. It has a revered statute of the Virgin Mary holding the infant Jesus whose healing powers attract thousands of pilgrims. Dating from 1489, the Gothic chapel features a richly decorated interior with a golden sunburst insignia above the altar and votive candles before the sacred Madonna statue. Pilgrims travel from across Germany and Europe to pray and leave offerings of flowers and petition notes asking for Mary's intervention and blessings. Because of its many miraculous legends, the Altötting shrine is known as the Lourdes of Germany.

# *Church of Maria Alm*

## **Austria**

The Church of Maria Alm is considered the most important pilgrimage place in Austria's Pinzgau region. First mentioned in historical documents in 1374, the church was rebuilt several times and became an independent parish in 1838. Incorporating both Baroque and Gothic architectural elements, with a steeple 84 metres in height, the church is famous for its miraculous statue of Mary holding the infant Jesus carved in 1636 and its frescoes dating from 1757.

# *Sanctuary of Madonna del Sasso*

## **Locarno • Switzerland**

High above Locarno, Switzerland, the Sanctuary of Madonna del Sasso is a breathtakingly beautiful sacred site. Founded in the 15th century, the sanctuary is named after an apparition of the Virgin Mary to Brother Bartolomeo in 1480. With its main holy structure dating back to the late 15th century, pilgrimages have continued since the sanctuary's inception. The Feast of the Assumption on 15 August marks the primary pilgrimage period, drawing visitors who are seeking solace and divine inspiration.

# *Church of Santa Rosalia*

## **Monte Pellegrino, Sicily • Italy**

The Church of Santa Rosalia, located on Monte Pellegrino in Sicily, Italy, was built in the 17th century in honour of Saint Rosalia, the patron saint of Palermo. It is famous for its cave sanctuary, believed to be where the saint lived in seclusion and ultimately died. Each year in July, an important feast known as the 'Festino' is celebrated in her honour.

# *S'Ena'e Thomes*

## Dorgali, Sardinia • Italy

In Sardinia, Italy, the enigmatic S'Ena'e Thomes dolmen beckons visitors seeking to explore its ancient roots. The site's significance lies in its connection to the prehistoric Nuragic culture, dating back to the 3rd millennium BCE. While no specific deity is associated with the site, it is believed to have served as a ceremonial and shamanic site. Although there are no particular pilgrimage periods associated with it, S'Ena'e Thomes continues to captivate visitors with its enduring mythological importance and mysterious origins.

# *Pecherska Monastery*

## **Kiev • Ukraine**

Kiev, Ukraine, is home to the Pecherska Monastery, a revered Eastern Orthodox Christian complex. Established as a cave monastery in 1051, this sacred site is known for its extensive underground caves, which house mummified monks and revered relics. The monastery has been a pilgrimage destination for centuries, with the most significant pilgrimage period occurring during the celebration of the Holy Dormition in August.

# *Monastery of Pochayiv*

## **Pochayiv • Ukraine**

The earliest historical record of the hilltop Monastery of Pochayiv in Ukraine dates from 1527, when, according to legend, the Virgin Mary appeared to monks in the shape of a column of fire, leaving her footprint on the rock upon which she stood. This imprint is revered for the medicinal properties of the water flowing from it. Today the monastery is the second most important pilgrimage site in Ukraine after the Monastery of the Caves in Kiev.

# *Voronet Monastery*

## Voronet • Romania

The Voronet Monastery, situated amidst the beautiful landscape of Romania, is often called the 'Sistine Chapel of the East' because of its vibrant frescoes that display stories from the Christian tradition. The monastery was established in 1488 and is devoted to St George, making it a significant place of worship for Orthodox Christians. During important religious holidays such as Easter and Christmas, the monastery experiences a surge in visitors, who gather to partake in communal prayer and celebrate these significant events.

# *Tekke of Sari Salltiku*

## **Mali i Krujës • Albania**

Established in the 14th century, the Tekke, or burial site, of Sari Salltiku in Mali i Krujës is the second most important pilgrimage site in Albania, after Mount Tomorr. A holy place of the Bektashi order, a Sufi branch of Islam, it is located in a cave near the summit of Sarisalltik mountain. Sari Salltiku was a revered 13th-century Sufi teacher. Pilgrims visit his cave shrine and holy spring throughout the year, with the busiest period in August during the saint's festival.

# *Shrine of Abu Zamaa al-Balawi*

## Kairouan • Tunisia

Approximately 1 km west of the Great Mosque of Kairouan, Tunisia, stands the Tomb of Abu Zamaa al-Balawi, a companion, or sahab, of the Prophet Muhammad. The tomb, called a zaouia or zawiya, is sometimes called the Mosque of the Barber because Abu Zamaa al-Balawi was believed to always carry three hairs from the beard of the Prophet Muhammad. While the original mausoleum dates from the 7th century, most of what stands today was added at the end of the 17th century.

# *Mount Oldonyo Lengai*

## **Tanzania**

Located in Tanzania, Mount Oldonyo Lengai, meaning Mountain of God, holds great significance in the Maasai culture. This revered site honours the Maasai deity, Engai, who is believed to reside within the volcano's crater. Rising to an altitude of 2,962 metres, it has long been a place of pilgrimage for Tanzania's pastoralists, who pray for the most essential elements in their world: rain, cattle and healthy children. In one of the more common rituals, Maasai elders lead groups of barren women to the mountain's base, where they pray to Engai to bless them with children.

# *Great Zimbabwe*

## Zimbabwe

Great Zimbabwe is an archaeological ruin in the south-eastern hills of Zimbabwe. Construction of the monument began in the 11th century and continued until the 15th. There are various mysteries surrounding Great Zimbabwe that orthodox archaeological interpretations cannot explain. Perhaps it was the capital of the Kingdom of Zimbabwe during the country's Late Iron Age, yet there are no burials anywhere near the vicinity of the ruins. And what was the purpose of the enigmatic hilltop complex above the primary ruins, which compelling evidence suggests was used as an astronomical observatory and ceremonial site?

# *Maqam Sidi Ahmed al-Badawi*

## Tanta • Egypt

Maqam Sidi Ahmed al-Badawi, located in Tanta, Egypt, and revered by Muslims and Christians alike, first became a place of pilgrimage in the 13th century. The main holy structure at the site is the *maqam*, or tomb, of the Moroccan Sufi Sidi Ahmed al-Badawi, who is considered a saint because of the many miracles he performed during his lifetime, in particular curing impotence and making barren women fertile. The main festival, attended by more than two million pilgrims, occurs during the *moulid* (celebration of the Prophet Muhammad's birthday) of Al-Sayed al-Badawi, celebrated annually in late October.

# *Church of the Virgin Mary*

## **Zeitoun • Egypt**

Zeitoun, Egypt, is home to the Coptic Church of the Virgin Mary. A series of miraculous appearances of the Virgin in the late 1960s sanctified this sacred Christian site. Pilgrims are drawn to the area throughout the year, particularly on the Feast of the Assumption in August. The church bears testimony to the enduring mythological importance of the Virgin Mary in Christianity.

## *Shrine of the Abdurrahman Gazi Mezarligi*

### **Erzurum • Turkey**

Located in the hills overlooking the city of Erzurum, Turkey, is the beautiful shrine of the Abdurrahman Gazi Mezarligi. One of the early leaders of the Ottoman Empire, famous as a brave and noble warrior, he died in 1329. His tomb was discovered in 1796 and has drawn pilgrims from throughout Turkey and the Middle East.

## *Shrine of Somuncu Baba*

### **Darende • Turkey**

The Sufi saint Somuncu Baba shrine is located 80 km northwest of Malatya, Turkey, near the town of Darende. Born in the 14th century, Somunca Baba was originally named Sheikh Hamid-I Wali. After studying across the Islamic world, he settled in Bursa, where he was known as the 'Father of Loaf' for his charity. He later moved to Darende and lived by a sacred spring where disciples visited him. Upon his death in 1412, this site became his pilgrimage shrine. In 1685 it was incorporated into a mosque and tomb complex. The sacred spring emanating from the cliffs has orange fish and a constant cool temperature. Inside are relics from Prophet Muhammad and the tombs of Somunca Baba and his son.

# *Tomb of Rabbi Isaac Luria*

## **Safed • Israel**

The cemetery of the city of Safed in Israel holds the Tomb of Rabbi Isaac Luria, renowned for his teachings on the Kabbalah, or Jewish mysticism. Pilgrimages to his tomb date back to the 16th century and there are thousands of other graves on the rocky hill. Every year hundreds of thousands of pilgrims visit the cemetery from Israel and abroad. Most of them come to pay homage to two graves: those of Rabbi Isaac Luria (Ha'Ari, 'The Lion') and Rabbi Joseph Karo.

# *Shrine of the Bab*

## **Haifa • Israel**

The Shrine of the Bab is a structure on the slopes of Mount Carmel in Haifa, Israel, which contains the Tomb of the Bab, the founder of the Bahá'í faith. It is considered the second holiest place on earth for Bahá'ís, after the Shrine of Bahá'u'lláh in Acre, Israel.

# *Franciscan Church of the Transfiguration*

## Mount Tabor • Israel

Perched atop Mount Tabor, 9 km east of Nazareth in Israel, the Franciscan Church of the Transfiguration commemorates Jesus' transfiguration before his disciples, when he spoke with Moses and Elijah. Established as a pilgrimage site in the 4th century, it holds deep significance for Christians. Constructed in the 1920s, the church stands upon Byzantine and Crusader ruins. Pilgrims journey here during the Feast of the Transfiguration in August.

MEVS DILECTVS

# *Church of the Assumption*

## Jerusalem • Israel

In Jerusalem, Israel, at the foot of the Mount of Olives and next to the Garden of Gethsemane, stands the Church of the Assumption, containing the crypt Tomb of Mary. Built 800 years ago, at the time of the Crusader Queen Melisende, it venerates the Dormition, the 'falling asleep' of the Virgin Mary, and her Assumption to Heaven. A popular sacred place throughout the year, the Feast of the Dormition on 15 August brings large numbers of pilgrims to the church.

# *Mausoleum of Hasan al-Basri*

## **Basra • Iraq**

The Mausoleum of Hasan al-Basri in downtown Basra, Iraq, houses the tomb of the revered 8th-century Islamic scholar and Sufi mystic known for his knowledge and piety. He died in 728 and his ornate mausoleum, featuring a large turquoise-tiled dome, was constructed 500 years later. Intricate arches and calligraphy surround Hasan al-Basri's tomb. Expanded over the centuries, the shrine receives Muslim pilgrims coming to pay their respects at the burial place of this important early saint.

# *Mausoleums of Imam Ali Alhadi and Imam Hasan Alaskari*

## **Samarra • Iraq**

Baghdad, Iraq, is home to the Mausoleum of Abdul Qadir Gilani. This esteemed site pays tribute to the life and teachings of the influential Sufi saint, Abdul Qadir Gilani. Pilgrimages to the mausoleum have been taking place since the 12th century. The main holy structure, a mosque and tomb complex, was built during the saint's lifetime. Pilgrims visit throughout the year, particularly during the annual *urs* (death anniversary) of Abdul Qadir Gilani.

الحسين الشهيد
علي زين العابدين
محمد الباقر
جعفر الصادق
موسى الكاظم

# *Mausoleum of Seventh Imam Musa al-Kadhim and Ninth Imam Muhammad al-Jawad*

## Kadhimiya, Baghdad • Iraq

The mausoleum in the Kadhimiya district of Baghdad, Iraq, houses the tombs of the revered Seventh and Ninth Shia Imams, Musa al-Kadhim and Muhammad al-Jawad. Built in 1515 (although this had been a pilgrimage site for many centuries), the elaborate mausoleum features a golden dome and intricate ornamentation. Its location in the largely Shia Kadhimiya neighbourhood draws hundreds of thousands of pilgrims annually, especially on holy days, to pray and mourn at the tombs of the Prophet Muhammad's descendants.

# *Mausoleum of al-Sharif al-Radhi*

## **Kadhimiya, Baghdad • Iraq**

The 16th-century Mausoleum of al-Sharif al-Radhi in the Kadhimiya district of Baghdad, Iraq, contains the ornate Iranian-tiled tomb of the eminent 10th-century Shia scholar–poet who served as an Abbasid vizier renowned for his patronage of poetry and the arts along with his religious knowledge. This important Shia pilgrimage site honouring the legacy of the revered descendant of Musa al-Kadhim features a complex including a mosque and library.

# *Mausoleum of Abdul Qadir Gilani*

## **Baghdad • Iraq**

Baghdad, Iraq, is home to the Mausoleum of Abdul Qadir Gilani. This esteemed site pays tribute to the life and teachings of the influential Sufi saint, Abdul Qadir Gilani. Pilgrimages to the mausoleum have been taking place since the 12th century. The main holy structure, a mosque and tomb complex, was built during the saint's lifetime. Pilgrims visit throughout the year, particularly during the annual *urs* (death anniversary) of Abdul Qadir Gilani.

# *The Mausoleum of Alqasim*

## **Babylon • Irak**

The Mausoleum of Alqasim is an ancient tomb located in the historical city of Babylon, Iraq. Built in the 9th century AD, it houses the remains of Alqasim Ibn Ubayd Allah, who ruled over the Abbasid Caliphate from 842 to 857 AD. The mausoleum is made of baked brick, and features elaborate geometric patterns and Arabic calligraphy decorating its exterior facade. Inside, Alqasim's sarcophagus lies beneath an ornate domed ceiling. The mausoleum is an excellent example of early Islamic architecture, combining stylistic elements from ancient Babylonian, Persian, and Central Asian traditions. Though battered by centuries of war and neglect, the Mausoleum of Alqasim still stands as an imposing monument to Iraq's rich cultural heritage.

# *The Shrines of Muslim ibn Aqeel and Hani ibn Urwa*

## **Kufa • Iraq**

The Shrines of Muslim ibn Aqeel and Hani ibn Urwa are two historic holy sites in Kufa, Iraq. Muslim ibn Aqeel was a prominent supporter of Imam Husayn, who was killed in Kufa in 680 CE, and a key figure in the events leading to the tragic battle of Karbala. Hani ibn Urwa offered Muslim refuge in his home, but both were eventually executed by forces of the Umayyad ruler Yazid I. Centuries later, shrines were built over their traditional burial sites to honor these martyrs of early Shi'a Islam, even though pilgrims have journeyed to this sacred destination since the 7th century. The Islamic month of Muharram always sees a surge in their numbers. The shrines feature golden domes and minarets with intricately decorated interiors. Despite damage from wars and extremist attacks, they remain important pilgrimage sites for Shi'a Muslims. The two shrines are enduring symbols of sacrifice and resilience in Kufa's historic Maidan district.

# *Mausoleum of Imam Hussein*

## **Karbala • Iraq**

The golden-domed Mausoleum of Imam Hussain in Karbala, Iraq, is a 19th-century Shia shrine housing the tomb of Hussain ibn Ali, grandson of the Prophet Muhammad and revered Third Imam martyred at the battle of Karbala in 680. Despite damage from bombings, this vital pilgrimage site draws millions of Shia pilgrims annually, especially during Ashura commemorations.

# *Mausoleum of Abbas*

## Karbala • Iraq

The Mausoleum of Abbas in Karbala, Iraq, houses the tomb of Abbas ibn Ali, revered Shia martyr and half-brother of Imam Hussain, slain at the battle of Karbala in 680. Abbas is honoured by Shias for sacrificing his life to save Hussain. First built in the 12th century, the current ornate golden-domed mausoleum dates to the 18th-century Safavid dynasty. Millions of pilgrims visit annually, especially during Ashura, to pay respects at Abbas's grave in one of Shia Islam's holiest cities.

# *Shrines of Zoroastrianism*

## **Chak Chak • Iran**

Chak Chak, located near Ardakan in central Iran, is the most sacred of the mountain shrines of Zoroastrianism. Each year from 14 to 18 June, thousands of Zoroastrians from Iran, India and other countries flock to the Fire Temple of Pir-e-Sabz. Tradition has it that pilgrims must stop riding when they catch sight of the temple and complete the last leg of their journey on foot.

# *Shrine of the Sufi saint Shah Nur-ed-Din Neatollah Vali*

**Mahan • Iran**

Located in south-central Iran, the small town of Mahan holds the beautiful pilgrimage shrine of the Sufi saint Shah Nur-ed-Din Nematollah Vali (1331–1431). Nematollah travelled widely in the Islamic world, studying with different scholars and sages before settling in Mahan in 1406 and founding a Sufi sect. The small room where he prayed and meditated contains beautiful tile decorations and has a wonderfully peaceful feeling.

# *Shrine of Imamzade Shah-e' Abdal-Azim*

## **Rey • Iran**

To the southeast of Tehran, just beyond that city's vast urban sprawl, lies the ancient city of Rey and its pilgrimage shrine of Shah-e' Abdal-Azim. Archaeological evidence indicates the city was important during the Achaemenian (559-330 BC) and Sassanian (224-637 AD) periods. Rey was occupied by the Muslims in 635 AD, was the regional capital in the 11th and 12th centuries, and was later plundered by Mongols in the 13th century. Within the large shrine complex are buried the religious scholar Shah Abdul Azim (786-865 AD), a descendant of Imam Hussein; Hamzeh, a brother of Imam Reza; Hussain, the great-grandson of the second Imam Hassan, and Taher, a descendant of the fourth Imam.

# *Mosque of Jam Karan*

## Jam Karan • Iran

Six kilometers east of the city of Qum stands the magnificent mosque of Jam Karan. In 986 AD, a devout Muslim by the name of Hassan ibn Muthlih had a mystical experience in which the Imam al-Mahdi (the Imam of the Ages, and son of the 11th Imam, al-Hasan al-Askari) and the prophet Khizr (the 'Green Sage') appeared to him and directed him to organize the building of a mosque on the holy ground of Jam Karan. The mosque was built by Sheikh Afif Saleh Hassan ibn Mosleh Jamkarani in 1006 and has attracted vast numbers of pilgrims since that time.

# *Mir Movsum Aga Mausoleum*

## **Baku • Azerbaijan**

An important spiritual site near Baku, Azerbaijan, the Mir Movsum Aga Mausoleum is dedicated to the memory of a revered 8th-century holy figure, Mir Movsum Aga. The existing structure, constructed in the 17th century, is a remarkable example of Islamic architecture, showing the intricate designs and artistry of the period. Particularly during Nowruz, the Persian New Year, many worshippers visit the mausoleum, believing that Mir Movsum Aga can grant miracles.

# *Temple of Garni*

## Armenia

The Temple of Garni is an iconic Greco-Roman structure in Garni, Armenia. Constructed in the 1st century, the ancient pagan temple is the best-preserved Hellenistic building in Armenia. Situated along the Azat River gorge, the architecture reflects Armenian craftsmanship applied to Classical styles. The temple features ornate 24-columned porticos, carvings of gods and goddesses, and an ancient sacrificial fire altar. Though pagan, the temple has become an Armenian spiritual symbol over the centuries.

# *Sulaiman Too*

## Osh • Kyrgyzstan

Sulaiman Too, a sacred mountain in Osh, Kyrgyzstan, has been revered for thousands of years. The main holy structure, a mosque, was constructed in the 16th century. Pilgrims from various religious traditions, including Islam and pre-Islamic beliefs, visit the site throughout the year. Its mythological importance stems from the belief that Sulaiman Too holds divine healing properties, drawing visitors seeking physical and spiritual restoration.

# *Mausoleum of Ismamut Ata*

## **Gorogly, Dashoguz • Turkmenistan**

The Mausoleum of Ismamut Ata in Gorogly, Dashoguz, Turkmenistan, is a venerated Islamic pilgrimage site dating back to the 11th century. Pilgrims visit throughout the year, with a particular emphasis on Islamic holidays. The mausoleum's importance is derived from Ismamut Ata, a respected Sufi spiritual leader who guided followers on their mystical journey.

# *Ak Ishan*

## **Ak Ishan • Turkmenistan**

Ak Ishan in Turkmenistan is an important Sufi pilgrimage site dedicated to Ak Ishan Baba, a revered 19th-century Sufi saint and healer. Visited by pilgrims throughout the year, it is especially popular during the religious festival of Nevruz at the time of the spring equinox.

# *Shrine of Baha al-Din al-Naqshbandi*

## **Bukhara • Uzbekistan**

Bukhara, Uzbekistan, is home to the revered Shrine of Baha al-Din al-Naqshbandi. Established in the 16th century, it pays tribute to the founder of the influential Naqshbandi Sufi order, Baha al-Din al-Naqshbandi. Pilgrims have revered this holy site for centuries, visiting all year round, particularly during Islamic holidays. The shrine's mythological importance lies in the teachings of Baha al-Din al-Naqshbandi, emphasising spiritual introspection and devotion to God.

# *Mausoleum of Khoja Ahmed Yasawi*

## Turkestan • Kazakhstan

Located in the city of Turkestan in southern Kazakhstan, the Mausoleum of Khoja Ahmed Yasawi honors the famous Turkic poet and Sufi mystic, Khoja Ahmed Yasawi (1093–1166). The structure was commissioned in 1389 by Timur, who ruled the area as part of the expansive Timurid Empire, to replace a smaller 12th-century tomb. The site draws pilgrims from across Central Asia.

# *Blue Mosque*

## Mazar-e-Sharif • Afghanistan

The Blue Mosque in Mazar-e-Sharif, Afghanistan, is an important Islamic holy site dedicated to the Prophet Muhammad's cousin, Ali ibn Abi Talib. Built during the late 15th century, it is renowned for its intricate blue-tiled mosaics. Pilgrims throughout Central Asia have journeyed to the Blue Mosque for centuries, with the most significant pilgrimage period being the Islamic month of Muharram.

# *Mausoleum of Shah Rukn-e-Alam*

## Multan • Pakistan

In Multan, Pakistan, the Mausoleum of Shah Rukn-e-Alam is a stunning example of Sufi architecture. Dedicated to the 14th-century Sufi saint, Shah Rukn-e-Alam, the mausoleum was built in the 14th century and has been a major pilgrimage site since its inception. Pilgrims primarily visit during the saint's *urs* (death anniversary), a celebration held annually.

# *Mausoleum of Hazrat Bahauddin Zakariya*

**Multan • Pakistan**

The Mausoleum of Hazrat Bahauddin Zakariya is an ornate 14th-century tomb shrine in Multan, Pakistan, honoring the eminent Sufi saint and spiritual leader. Through his mystical teachings, Zakariya played a pivotal role in spreading Islam in South Asia during the 13th century. Today, this intricately decorated shrine complex with its distinctive turquoise dome attracts thousands of devotees, especially during the annual Urs festival commemorating the death anniversary of this influential Sufi saint. The tomb's architectural beauty and enduring spiritual allure reflect Hazrat Bahauddin Zakariya's lofty status as one of South Asia's most revered Sufi saints.

# *Varasidhi Vinayaka Swamy Temple*

## **Kanipakam, Andhra Pradesh • India**

The 11th-century Varasidhi Vinayaka Swamy temple in Kanipakam, Andhra Pradesh, India, is devoted to Ganesh, the Hindu god of wisdom and prosperity. The annual Ganesh Chaturthi festival draws a multitude of devotees seeking the blessings of the deity for success, wisdom, and the removal of all obstacles.

# *Veerabhadra Swamy Temple*

## **Lepakshi, Andhra Pradesh • India**

Veerabhadra Swamy Temple, nestled in the historic town of Lepakshi, Andhra Pradesh, India, is dedicated to the powerful manifestation of Lord Shiva as Veerabhadra. Built during the Vijayanagara period in the 16th century, the temple is renowned for its intricate carvings, soaring pillars and architectural splendour. Maha Shivaratri is the primary pilgrimage period when tens of thousands of devotees flock to the temple to immerse themselves in the potent spiritual energy and pay homage to Veerabhadra.

# *Sivadol Temple*

## Sivasagar, Assam • India

The famous trio of 18th-century Hindu temples called Sivadol, Visnudol and Devidol are situated in Sivasagar, Assam, India, about 370 km east of Guwahati. Constructed on the artificial Borpukhuri Lake by Ahom queen Ambika, these temples dedicated to Shiva, Vishnu and Durga reflect the Ahom dynasty's architectural style. The 104-foot-tall Sivadol contains a uniquely inverted Shiva lingam and is considered India's tallest Shiva temple. Along with the other temples, this complex attracts hundreds of thousands of pilgrims annually for major festivals like Shivratri, Janmashtami, Durga Puja and Rath Yatra. With roots dating back to the 13th century Ahoms, the temples exemplify Assamese history while remaining active pilgrimage sites.

# *Surya Pahar*

## **Assam • India**

Surya Pahar, located near the Brahmaputra River in Assam, India, was an important Hindu, Buddhist and Jain pilgrimage site from the 1st century BCE until its decline in the 13th century CE. In the 1st century BCE, Hinayana Buddhists began carving religious symbols on the granite hillside. In the 9th century CE, Hindus and Jains added temples, like the partially excavated Panchayatana Temple dedicated to Surya, the sun god. Hundreds of carved Shiva lingams are scattered across the sacred hill, reflecting its significance to Hindus. After fading in popularity, a 20th-century Surya temple revived pilgrimages somewhat. However, excavations in the 2000s uncovered artefacts affirming the spiritual importance of Surya Pahar, with its carved imagery and ruins, from antiquity through the medieval period.

# *Tilinga Mandir*

## **Bordubi, Assam • India**

Located in Bordubi, Assam, India, Tilinga Mandir is a unique temple devoted to Shiva. In the 1960s, the temple emerged as a pilgrimage site after a farmer's dream of a divine presence beneath a tree. The temple's most striking feature are the countless hanging bells that devotees offer so that their wishes may be fulfilled. The major pilgrimage period is the month of Shravan, during which the temple witnesses an influx of devotees.

# *Mandar Hill*

## **Bihar • India**

Mandar Hill is a small yet sacred granite hill around 213 metres high located in Bihar's Banka district in India. In Hindu lore, it is revered for its connection to Samudra Manthan – the legend of the 'churning of the ocean' by gods and demons in which Mandar Hill served as the churning rod. Owing to this mythic significance, the hilltop is home to Hindu temples like Someshwar Mahadev with its Shiva Kapilash lingam. Scattered with sacred water tanks and shrines to other deities, Mandar Hill attracts thousands of pilgrims who perform religious rituals during major festivals. Its panoramic views and spiritual aura from Hindu mythology have established Mandar Hill as a key pilgrimage site in Bihar.

# *Mundeshwari Devi Temple*

## Bihar • India

Mundeshwari Devi Temple is an ancient Hindu shrine located in Bihar, India, believed to have been constructed between 625 and 850 in the Nagara architectural style. Dedicated to the goddess Mundeshwari Devi, an incarnation of Kali, its inner sanctum houses her four-armed image and a Shiva lingam. Inscriptions in Brahmi script provide historical details about its construction under the patronage of Shahi, Kushan and Gupta dynasty rulers between the 6th and 8th centuries. The temple complex also contains the ruins of several subsidiary shrines. As one of the oldest intact Hindu temples in eastern India, Mundeshwari Devi Temple is of immense archaeological and religious significance.

মা

# *Maa Bamleshwari Temple*

## Chhattisgarh • India

Maa Bamleshwari Temple in the state of Chhattisgarh, India, is dedicated to the goddess Bamleshwari, an incarnation of Durga, and is also one of the famous Shakti Peetha shrines. Though its origins may date back to the 7th century, the current medieval-style temple was built in the 18th century. The inner sanctum contains the stone idol of the 18-armed Bamleshwari riding a tiger. The temple complex also has shrines to other deities. As the most famous temple in Chhattisgarh, it received historic patronage from regional rulers and still draws millions of Hindu pilgrims annually, especially during the Dussehra and Navaratri festivals in late September and October.

# *Chamunda Devi Temple*

## Himachal Pradesh • India

Perched on a hilltop overlooking the Banganga and Manjhi rivers near Dharamshala, Himachal Pradesh, India, Chamunda Devi Temple is dedicated to the Hindu goddess Chamunda, a fierce incarnation of Durga. Believed to have been constructed around the 10th century, with its current structure dating to the 17th century, the temple features ornate stone carvings, pinnacles, and a dome over the inner sanctum housing the statue of the goddess. The complex also contains shrines to Shiva, Hanuman and Narsingh. As a highly popular Shakti pilgrimage site, it draws thousands of devotees annually, especially during Navaratri celebrations.

# *Renuka Temple*

## Himachal Pradesh • India

Renuka Temple, built in 1814 on the shore of a serene mountain lake, is located in Himachal Pradesh, India. In ancient times, according to legend, the sage Jamadagni and his wife Renuka, an incarnation of the goddess Durga, used to meditate and pray on a hill overlooking the lake. Because of the couple's devotion, they gave birth to a son named Parashurama, considered an incarnation of the god Vishnu. It is said that Parshurama wished to spend his life at his mother's feet, and it is because of this that the mother–son duo meets every year during the annual Renuka fair. Pilgrims have visited the temple since the 18th century to worship the goddess and seek blessings.

शिव मन्दिर
मन्दिर माता रेणुका जी

# *Baba Garib Nath Temple*

## **Himachal Pradesh • India**

Nestled in Himachal Pradesh, India, Baba Garib Nath Temple is dedicated to the Hindu sage, Baba Garib Nath. This shrine has been a place of pilgrimage since the 17th century. The main holy structure attracts devotees all year round, especially during the vibrant Sawan month. Believed to grant the wishes of childless couples, the temple holds mythological importance as the dwelling place of the sage, who is said to have divine powers.

# *Mahaganapati Temple*

## Gokarna, Karnataka • India

Mahaganapati Temple in Gokarna, Karnataka, India, on the Arabian Sea, was first used as a place of pilgrimage in the 4th century. The temple contains a statue of the Hindu deity Ganesha, considered to be the remover of obstacles and the lord of new beginnings. The primary pilgrimage periods are during the annual Chaturthi and Shivaratri festivals. The site is of mythological importance as it is believed that Lord Ganesha was born in this region and that the temple was built to commemorate his birthplace. One hundred metres away is the equally important Mahabaleshwar Shiva Temple.

# *Talakaveri Temple*

## **Karnataka • India**

Talakaveri Temple, located in Karnataka, India, is a sacred site at the mouth of the revered Kaveri River. Dedicated to the river goddess Kaveri, the temple complex is believed to be more than 2,000 years old. During the Tula Sankramana festival, thousands of devotees gather to witness the sudden upsurge of the holy spring and to seek blessings for their prosperity and well-being.

# *Mahaganapathi Temple*

## Madhur, Kerala • India

Mahaganapathi Temple is a major 16th-century Hindu temple situated amid lush greenery on the banks of the Madhura Puzha River in Kerala, India. While legends trace its origins back to a much earlier period, the temple was constructed in the 16th century and is considered one of Kerala's most revered Ganesh shrines. Its presiding deity is a massive 16-foot granite sculpture of seated Ganesh known as Mahaganapathi Moorthi housed in the inner sanctum of this architecturally striking Kerala-style temple complex that covers 7 walled acres. Daily rituals are conducted by priests, and major festivals draw large crowds of Hindu pilgrims seeking blessings, especially during the annual 10-day Mahotsav celebrations in December.

# *Guruvayur Krishna Temple*

## **Kerala • India**

One of the most sacred Hindu temples dedicated to Lord Krishna is Guruvayur Krishna Temple in Kerala, India. Believed to be over 5,000 years old, with legends dating to the 16th century, the main deity is Lord Krishna as a four-armed black stone idol. Millions are drawn to Guruvayur, considered the Dwarka of the South, to offer prayers, flowers and oils and perform rituals at elaborately carved shrines like the famous Guruvayurappan Chittambalam, where Krishna is put to sleep every night. The temple hosts spectacular processions of the deity on elephants during festivals like Janmashtami that draw huge crowds.

# *Sabarimala Temple*

## **Kerala • India**

In the Indian state of Kerala, the early Dravidian people worshipped Ayappa, a youthful forest god born from the union of Shiva and Vishnu. Legends recount Shiva mating with Mohini, Vishnu's female incarnation, which produced Ayappa, an avatar sent to battle hill-tribe demons. Raised by a childless king, Ayappa performed miracles and healed people before disappearing into Sabarimala Temple in the mountain jungles. For a thousand years, mystics have reported seeing Ayappa riding tigers in the dense forests surrounding Sabarimala. Despite its remote setting, the shrine draws millions of devotees, who undergo 41 days of austerity before journeying through the mountains for a brief glimpse of the deity. To respect Ayappa's celibacy, however, women between the ages of 6 and 60 are not permitted.

# *Khandoba Marthanda Bhairava Temple*

## Jejuri, Maharashtra • India

Khandoba Marthanda Bhairava Temple in Jejuri, Maharashtra, India, is an important Hindu shrine dedicated to the fierce deity Khandoba, revered as a form of Shiva. Situated atop a steep hill, the temple complex has stunning architecture, intricately carved doorways and images of Khandoba riding a horse. The inner sanctum of the temple houses the Marthanda Bhairava statue of Khandoba. Thousands of devotees visit during major festivals, when the statue of Khandoba is taken on a grand procession. Especially on weekends, the hill resounds with the chanting of 'Shri Khandoba Jai Malhari'. People also seek blessings by offering coconuts, jewellery and large amounts of turmeric at the temple.

# *Tulja Bhavani Mandir*

## **Tuljapur, Maharashtra • India**

Tulja Bhavani Temple in Tuljapur, Maharashtra, India, is one of the 51 Shakti Peethas dedicated to the Hindu goddess Tulja Bhavani, a local form of Durga. The temple's origins can be traced back to the 12th century. The goddess Tulja Bhavani is manifested here as a *swayambhu* (naturally formed) image holding weapons and ornaments. Daily rituals involve adorning the statue of the goddess with silk clothing and elaborate floral decorations. The atmosphere comes alive during festivals like Chaitra Pournimaa when the statue is taken on procession. The temple attracts thousands of pilgrims seeking blessings and has received royal patronage from generations of rulers.

# *Ramkund*

## **Nashik, Maharashtra • India**

The sacred site of Ramkund in Nashik, Maharashtra, India, is home to an important ritual immersion site along the banks of the holy Godavari River. With strong connections to the Hindu epic the Ramayana, Lord Rama is believed to have bathed in these waters during his 14-year exile. Every 12 years, the renowned Kumbh Mela pilgrimage takes place, drawing millions of devotees seeking spiritual cleansing and divine blessings. The atmosphere surrounding the site makes it an ideal spot for meditation and reflection.

# *Great Stupa*

## Sanchi, Madhya Pradesh • India

Sanchi, a small town in Madhya Pradesh, India, has around 50 Buddhist monuments dating from the third century BCE to the twelfth century CE. The present Great Stupa (17 metres tall) is not the original but encases an earlier stupa. Contrary to popular belief, the Great Stupa contains no relics of the Buddha but only those of his disciples, Sariputra and Mahamoggallena.

# *Huma Leaning Temple*

## **Odisha • India**

The Leaning Temple of Huma in Odisha, India, is dedicated to the Hindu deity Lord Shiva and is known for its precarious tilted structure, much like the Leaning Tower of Pisa. Constructed in the early 16th century during Barga rule, the temple has tilted around 14 metres from its original position due to the sandy soil on the banks of the Mahanadi River. The temple follows classic Odisha architecture, with a Shiva lingam enshrined in the main sanctum. Despite being tilted, the temple has never collapsed and remains completely intact, adding to its allure and intrigue. While engineering factors like the sandy soil cause the tilt, local legends attribute it to the will of Lord Shiva. The miraculous leaning temple continues to stand today as an iconic Shiva shrine.

# *Siddha Jagannath Temple*

## **Odisha • India**

Siddha Jagannath Temple is an important Hindu shrine located some 2 km from the famous Jagannath Temple in Puri, Odisha, India. Built around the 12th century at the same time as Jagannath Temple, it is known as the 'perfect and complete' abode of Lord Jagannath, an avatar (incarnation) of Vishnu. The temple architecture showcases the Kalinga style with a 23-metre-tall vimana towering above the inner sanctum. The temple follows rituals established by Adi Shankaracharya and celebrates major festivals like Rath Yatra. Siddha Jagannath Temple stands as an integral counterpart to the main Jagannath shrine, representing the perfect completion of the Lord's abode in the holy city of Puri.

# *Maa Tara Tarini Temple*

## **Purushottampour, Odisha • India**

Maa Tara Tarini Temple, located in Purushottampur, Odisha, India, is a revered pilgrimage site dedicated to the worship of the goddesses of Shakti, Tara and Tarini. This ancient temple, with origins tracing back to the 6th century, serves as a hub for devotees seeking the goddesses' protection and blessings. The Chaitra Parva festival attracts thousands of pilgrims who engage in elaborate rituals, hoping to absorb the powerful energy that emanates from this spiritual sanctuary.

# *Willong Khullen*

## Manipur • India

Located in the remote mountains of northern Manipur, India, the magnificent collection of standing stones of Willong Khullen is one of the most mysterious and unstudied sacred places in the entire world. There are approximately 150 standing stones, many as tall as 27 metres, and absolutely nothing is known about them. Where the stones are from, who carved them, how they were transported to this site, how they were used and when the site was constructed … all of these are mysteries yet to be solved.

# *Kapil Muni Temple*

## West Bengal • India

Kapil Muni Temple is an ancient Hindu shrine in Sagar Island, West Bengal, India. Dedicated to the revered sage Kapil Muni, who is said to have lived and meditated here, the temple complex near the Ganges and Bay of Bengal confluence contains shrines and monasteries. The main temple is built in a Bengali architectural style, housing an idol of Kapil Muni in a seated, meditative pose. Legend has it that King Sagar's 60,000 sons were reduced to ashes here by Kapil Muni's angry gaze. Every year on 14 and 15 January, hundreds of thousands of Hindu pilgrims gather for a holy dip during Makar Sankranti's Gangasagar Mela.

# *Shiva Natraja Temple*

## **Chidambaram, Tamil Nadu • India**

Chidambaram, Tamil Nadu, India, is home to the illustrious Shiva Natraja Temple. Dedicated to Lord Shiva, this ancient temple is renowned for depicting Shiva's cosmic dance, the Nataraja. With origins tracing back to the 10th century, the temple remains a significant pilgrimage site and large numbers of pilgrims arrive during the annual Margazhi and Aani Thirumanjanam festivals. The temple's mythological essence lies in Shiva's dance, representing creation, preservation and destruction.

# *Arulmigu Patteswar Swamy Temple*

## Coimbatore, Tamil Nadu • India

Arulmigu Patteswar Swamy Temple, located in Coimbatore, Tamil Nadu, India, is an important spiritual site dedicated to Shiva and his consort Parvati. Constructed during the 9th century by the Chola dynasty, this temple is famous for its architectural magnificence, intricate carvings and expansive courtyards. The annual Maha Shivaratri festival attracts a multitude of devotees.

# *Saranatha Perumal Vishnu Temple*

## Tirucherai, Tamil Nadu • India

The captivating Saranatha Perumal Vishnu Temple, situated in Tirucherai, Tamil Nadu, India, is an important pilgrimage site for the worship of the Hindu god Vishnu. With a rich history dating back more than 1,000 years, the temple's distinctive five-tiered rajagopuram (gateway tower) is an architectural marvel. During the primary pilgrimage period of Vaikuntha Ekadashi, devotees throng to the temple to pay their respects, seek divine intervention and immerse themselves in the powerful spiritual atmosphere.

# *Sri Jogulamba Ammavari Temple*

## **Alampur, Telangana • India**

Sri Jogulamba Ammavari Temple, situated in Alampur, Telangana, India, is a highly important Shakti Peetha dedicated to the fierce goddess Jogulamba. With a history spanning over a millennium, the temple is revered as one of the 18 Maha Shakti Peethas and represents a potent source of divine energy. During special occasions like Navratri, the temple comes alive with fervent devotion as throngs of worshippers converge to seek the goddess's blessings for protection, wisdom and abundance in their lives.

رسول الله

# *Gorakhnath Temple*

## **Gorakhpur, Uttar Pradesh • India**

Gorakhpur, Uttar Pradesh, India, features the esteemed Gorakhnath Temple, which celebrates the revered yogi, Gorakhnath. The temple's origins can be traced back to the 11th century and it continues to draw pilgrims today. Devotees gather in large numbers during the Makar Sankranti and Khichdi festivals.

# *Tomb and Shrine of Kabir*

## **Magahar, Uttar Pradesh • India**

Magahar, Uttar Pradesh, India, is home to the Tomb and Shrine of Kabir (1398–1518), a legendary poet and mystic who preached religious tolerance and universal love. Established in the 16th century, the shrine is an important pilgrimage destination for Kabir's followers and lovers of mystical poetry.

# *Chakra Tirtha*

## **Naimisharanya, Uttar Pradesh • India**

Chakra Tirtha, situated in Naimisharanya, Uttar Pradesh, India, is a sacred site linked to the divine chakra (disc or wheel) of Lord Vishnu. Pilgrims visit all year round, particularly during auspicious occasions like Somvati Amavasya. The site's mythological importance lies in the belief that Lord Vishnu's chakra created a lake, Naimisharanya, where sages practised meditation.

# *Hanuman Garhi Temple*

## **Naimisharanya, Uttar Pradesh • India**

Hanuman Garhi Temple in Naimisharanya, Uttar Pradesh, India, is a sacred space dedicated to Lord Hanuman. Believed to have been established by sages in ancient times, this temple is a testimony to Hanuman's devotion to Lord Rama. Pilgrims visit throughout the year, especially on Tuesdays and during Hanuman Jayanti.

## *Mahaparinirvana Stupa*

### **Kushinagar, Uttar Pradesh • India**

In Kushinagar, Uttar Pradesh, India, Mahaparinirvana Stupa is a testament to Buddha's passing into nirvana. Established as a pilgrimage site around the 5th century CE, the present temple was built by the Indian government in 1956 and it attracts Buddhist pilgrims from around the world. Inside the temple is a 6-metre-long reclining Buddha image lying on its right side.

# *Kedarnath Temple*

## **Uttarakhand • India**

Kedarnath Temple, located at 3,583 metres in the Himalayas in Uttarakhand, India, is one of Hinduism's most important pilgrimage sites. One of the four directional sacred places (Char Dham), as well as being one of the twelve most sacred Shiva temples (Jyotir Linga), it has attracted huge numbers of visitors since at least the 8th century, though only during May to October when the snows melt and the weather warms.

# *Makhdoom Sahib Dargah*

## **Srinagar, Kashmir • India**

Srinagar, Kashmir, India, is home to the sacred Makhdoom Sahib Dargah. Commemorating the revered 16th-century Sufi saint Makhdoom Sahib, this shrine has long been a pilgrimage destination for both Muslims and Hindus. Constructed in the 17th century, the central holy structure sits atop Hari Parbat Hill. The dargah's mythological importance stems from the saint's teachings, promoting peace and unity.

# *Amarnath Temple*

## Kashmir • India

Amarnath Temple is a Hindu shrine dedicated to Shiva in the state of Kashmir, in India. Situated inside a remote cave at an altitude of 3,888 metres, it is surrounded by glaciers and covered with snow for most of the year except for a short period in the summer, when it is open to pilgrims. A towering ice stalagmite in the cave, which represents Shiva, has attracted devotees for thousands of years, and nowadays more than 500,000 pilgrims walk to the temple each year. The cave is also considered a Shakti Peetha temple, one of 51 places on the Indian subcontinent that commemorate the location of fallen body parts of the Hindu deity Sati, the first wife of Shiva.

जय बाबा
भूखे को

# *Nagadeepa Purana Rajamaha Viharaya*

## **Nainathevu island • Sri Lanka**

Nagadeepa Purana Rajamaha Viharaya, situated on Nainathevu island in Sri Lanka, is an important Buddhist pilgrimage site believed to have been established around the 2nd century BCE. The temple venerates the Serpent King Cobra, who is said to have protected Lord Buddha during his meditation and second visit to Sri Lanka. Thousands of devotees visit the site annually, mainly from February to April.

# *Muktinath Temple*

## Nepal

Located high in the mountains (at 3,710 metres) in eastern Nepal, Muktinath Temple is a sacred site revered by both Hindus and Buddhists, who believe that bathing in its holy waters can bring spiritual liberation. Dating to the 12th century, it is one of the 108 holy places of Vishnu, one of 51 Shakti Peetha goddess sites, a sacred place of the Buddhist Dakini Sky Dancer goddesses, and one of the 24 Tantric places. Additionally, the site is considered to be a manifestation of Avalokiteshvara, the bodhisattva of compassion and virtue.

# *Janakpuri Temple*

## Janakpur • Nepal

Famous since the 8th century, Janakpuri Temple in Nepal is an important Hindu pilgrimage site dedicated to Sita. According to legend, Sita was born and married to Rama in Janakpur. The main temple, Janaki Mandir, was built in 1911 and attracts large numbers of pilgrims on such festivals as Ram Navami, the birthday of Rami in March or April; Vivah Panchami, the wedding day of Sita and Ram in November; Holi, the festival of colours in March; and Diwali, the festival of lights in early November.

# *Budanilkantha*

## **Kathmandu • Nepal**

Budanilkantha, located in Kathmandu, Nepal, is an enigmatic Hindu temple featuring a large, reclining statue of Lord Vishnu. This ancient site is believed to have been established around the 7th century. Devotees of Lord Vishnu flock to the temple primarily during the Haribodhini Ekadashi festival in October or November. The temple's mythological importance is connected to the legend of Lord Vishnu's slumber on the cosmic ocean, symbolising the creation and preservation of the universe.

# *Chimi Lhakhang Temple*

## Punakha district • Bhutan

Chimi Lhakhang Temple, also known as the Fertility Temple, is an important Buddhist monastery in the Punakha district of Bhutan. It was built in the 15th century by Lama Drukpa Kunley, an eccentric Buddhist saint known for promoting fertility. The temple is renowned for blessing childless couples with offspring, and an image of the saint's 'divine madman' phallus is worshipped here. The fertility shrine receives thousands of visitors annually seeking its blessings. Local women come to receive an auspicious tap from a wooden phallus. An embodiment of Buddhist beliefs and fertility traditions, Chimi Lhakhang is one of Bhutan's most distinct sacred sites.

# *Monastery of Tharpaling*

## **Bhutan**

The Monastery of Tharpaling (meaning 'the land of liberation') in Bhutan is associated with the Nyingma tradition and was established by the great Buddhist teacher Gyalwang Longchen Rabjampa in the 14th century. Devotees visit the monastery during the annual Tharpaling Tsechu festival, which typically falls in February.

# *Buli Goempa Monastery*

## Bhutan

Affiliated to the Nyingma tradition of Tibetan Buddhism, the secluded Buli Goempa Monastery in Bhutan was established in the 14th century by the Buddhist teacher, Terton Dorji Lingpa.

# *Kurjey Lhakhang*

## **Bumthang • Bhutan**

Kurjey Lhakhang, located in Bumthang, Bhutan, is a sacred complex containing three Buddhist temples. Established around the 8th century, this site is closely associated with Guru Rinpoche (Padmasambhava), who introduced Buddhism to Bhutan. Kurjey Lhakhang is most visited during the annual Kurjey Tsechu festival in June or July. Its mythological importance is rooted in the belief that Guru Rinpoche defeated a local demon here, imprinting his body's image on a rock.

# *Demchig Hiid Monastery*

## Mongolia

Established in Mongolia in the 17th century by the revered saint Öndör Gegeen Zanabazar (also a great sculptor, diplomat, painter and poet), Demchig Hiid Monastery was dedicated to the practice of Vajrayana Buddhism; its chief deity was Demchog, also known as Chakrasamvara. Mostly destroyed during the Stalinist purges in the 1930s, it has since been restored and is now a functioning monastery visited by pilgrims from throughout Buddhist Asia.

# *Tuvkhun Monastery*

## **Shireet Ulaan Uul • Mongolia**

Tuvkhun Monastery, perched at 2600 meters on Shireet Ulaan Uul mountain in Mongolia, was another monastery established in the 17th century by Öndör Gegeen Zanabazar. Originally called Bayasgalant Aglag Oron (Happy Secluded Place), it was his retreat for 30 years and where he created many of his most famous works of art. Destroyed during the Stalinist purges of the 1930s, it has since been reconstructed and is a functioning monastery and pilgrimage destination today.

# *Han Bogd Hairham*

## Mongolia

Mongolian shamanism, called Tengerism, refers to the animistic and shamanic religion practised in Mongolia since ancient times. It was tied to the social life and tribal organisation of Mongolian society and, over many centuries, was influenced by and mingled with Buddhism. The sacred mountain of Han Bogd Hairham, a place for worship of the Tengri sky deity marked by a distinctive stone monument adorned with ancient inscriptions and carvings, is highly venerated by pilgrims.

# *Galvan Zuu Temple*

## Tsetserleg • Mongolia

Overlooking the town of Tsetserleg, the capital of Arkhangai province in Mongolia, stands the sacred mountain of Zayin Horee and Galvan Zuu Temple. Hundreds of steps lead past the 7-metre-tall statue of Buddha to the temple, and there are numerous religious paintings and carvings on the rocks of the mountain. Believed to be inhabited by powerful spirits, the mountain is visited all year long, especially during the warmer summer months.

# *Monastery of Toling*

## **Tibet**

Located in south-western Tibet, the Monastery of Toling is a captivating sacred site that showcases a rich repository of Buddhist art and culture. Dating from the 10th century, this ancient monastery was once a prominent spiritual centre for the Guge Kingdom. Although there is no specific pilgrimage period, visiting during the Saga Dawa festival in May or June is especially exciting due to the large numbers of pilgrims.

# *Puji Si Temple*

## Pu Tuo Shan • China

Puji Si Temple, located on the mountainous island of Pu Tuo Shan in China, is a remarkable Buddhist temple dedicated to Guanyin, the bodhisattva of compassion, who, according to legend, attained enlightenment on the island. Founded during the Tang dynasty (618–907), the temple is believed to be the oldest wooden temple in the world. Pu Tuo Shan is considered one of the Four Sacred Mountains of Chinese Buddhism.

# *Saoba Stone Pillars*

## Ruisui • Taiwan

The Saoba Stone Pillars (also known as the Wuhe Stone Pillars), located near Ruisui, Taiwan, are a set of enigmatic megaliths that hold cultural significance for the indigenous Amis tribe, who use them to honour their ancestral spirits. Perhaps originally erected by the Beinan culture some 2,000–3,000 years ago and standing 5.75 and 3.99 metres in height, the megaliths may have been part of a larger complex of standing stones used to conduct horizon-based celestial observations for ceremonial purposes.

# *Chaotian Temple*

## **Beigang • Taiwan**

Chaotian Temple, located in Beigang, Taiwan, is a vibrant centre of worship dedicated to the revered goddess Mazu, the protector of seafarers. Established during the Qing dynasty in the early 18th century, this spiritual sanctuary boasts an exquisite blend of intricate carvings, delicate paintings and architectural elegance. The annual Mazu pilgrimage, one of Taiwan's largest religious events, draws a massive influx of devotees seeking protection, guidance and blessings from the beloved goddess.

# *Fo Guang Shan Temple*

## **Kaohsiung • Taiwan**

Fo Guang Shan Temple, near Kaohsiung, Taiwan, is a magnificent Buddhist monastery established in 1967 by Master Hsing Yun. The site contains the world's tallest bronze sitting Buddha statue, eight pagodas, thousands of Buddha and Guanyin statues, a tooth relic of the Buddha and facilities for visiting pilgrims. Numerous festivals are celebrated here throughout the year.

# *Cave Temple of Sanbangsa*

## Jeju Island • South Korea

Some 97 km off the south-western corner of the Korean peninsula stands the island of Jeju Island, dominated by the sacred mountain of Halla San (1,950 metres). White Deer Lake, in the crater at the top of the mountain, is said to be the abode of angelic presences. On the mountain's lower slope is the Cave Temple of Sanbangsa, once a pagan shrine, now a Buddhist sanctuary. Inside the cave is a pool of water believed to have healing and prayer-granting powers. Near the cave is a temple with many old statues of Buddha, which were brought to Jeju Island by pilgrims from many parts of South-East Asia during the past 1,000 years.

## *Hwaeomsa Monastery*

### **Mount Jirisan • South Korea**

Located on Mount Jirisan in South Korea, Hwaeomsa Monastery is a remarkable Buddhist temple dating from the 6th century. The temple is home to the magnificent Gakhwangjeon Hall, built in 1701. Although the monastery attracts pilgrims all year round, the peak pilgrimage period is during the annual Lotus Lantern festival, held in May. Hwaeomsa Monastery's mythological importance lies in its dedication to the Avatamsaka sutra, a foundational Buddhist text, and the Vairocana Buddha, who embodies the dharmakaya, or the truth body of the Buddha.

# *Taebaek-san*

## South Korea

Taebaek-san, the 'Grand White Mountain', is one of South Korea's holiest mountains, with important shamanic shrines and Buddhist temples. Each year on 3 October, the spectacular Cheonje ceremony is held on the mountain's summit to celebrate the nation's founding in 2333 BCE. The ceremony's mythological importance is attributed to the belief that it connects the earthly realm with the celestial realm, ensuring harmony and balance.

# *Chùa Bà Thiên Hâu Pagoda*

## **Saigon • Vietnam**

Chùa Bà Thiên Hâu is an expansive Buddhist pagoda complex located along the Hau River in Vietnam that was built in the early 19th century to honor Mazu, the Goddess of Mercy, known as Bà Thiên Hâu in Vietnamese. Sprawling over several hectares, it contains multiple temple structures, gardens, and courtyards, including the main pagoda featuring intricate carvings and a large statue of the goddess. The grounds also have shrines, Buddha images, bonsai gardens, tortoise lakes, and statuary set amidst lush greenery. Considered highly sacred, the pagoda attracts Buddhist pilgrims who come to pray, make offerings and seek blessings, especially during the annual Poya festival when thousands gather to participate in rituals honoring Bà Thiên Hâu.

# *Thien Mu Pagoda*

## **Hue • Vietnam**

Hue, Vietnam, is home to the ancient Thien Mu Pagoda, an iconic Buddhist temple known for its seven-story pagoda. Established in 1601, it has been a sacred place of pilgrimage for centuries. The temple's main structure, the Phuoc Duyen Tower, was built in 1844. The Thien Mu Pagoda's mythological significance is connected to the 'Celestial Lady,' a mystical figure believed to have appeared on a hill and prophesied the temple's construction.

# *Koh Ker*

## Cambodia

Koh Ker is a remote archaeological site in northern Cambodia, located 120 km from the ancient site of Angkor. More than 180 sanctuaries have been found in a protected area of 81 sq. km. Only about two dozen monuments can be visited because most of the sanctuaries are hidden in the forest and the area is not fully demined. Unparalleled in the Khmer civilisation is the 36-metre-high, seven-tiered Prang pyramid, which probably served as the state temple of Jayavarman IV, who ruled the site from 928 to 941 CE.

# *Wat Phabat Phonsane*

## Phabath • Laos

Nestled in Phabath, Laos, Wat Phabat Phonsane is a serene Buddhist temple that has been a pilgrimage site since the 16th century. Its most remarkable feature is the sacred 'footprint' of the Buddha, housed within the temple. This site remains an important spiritual destination for Buddhists seeking blessings and guidance. The main holy structure was built in 1620, while the temple complex has expanded over time. Pilgrims flock to the temple during the annual Wat Phabat Phonsane Festival, held in January. The site's mythological importance is tied to the belief that the Buddha's sacred footprint blesses all those who visit.

# *That Sikhottabong Stupa*

## Thakhek • Laos

Situated next to the Mekong River in Thakhek, Laos, That Sikhottabong Stupa is a revered Buddhist site dating back to the 6th century. Rising to 29 metres, it contains relics of the Buddha and is the scene of a multi-day pilgrimage each year on the full moon of the third lunar calendar (usually in February).

# *Shwe Mawdaw Pagoda*

## Bago • Myanmar

Bago, Myanmar, hosts the magnificent Shwe Mawdaw Pagoda, the tallest in Myanmar (114 metres). Initially constructed in the 10th century and destroyed several times due to earthquakes, it is believed to enshrine two sacred hairs of the Buddha. The Shwe Mawdaw Pagoda festival, held annually in April, is the primary pilgrimage period, though the site attracts pilgrims throughout the year.

# *Candi Sukuh*

## Mount Lawu • Java, Indonesia

Set against Mount Lawu in Java, Indonesia, Candi Sukuh is a sacred site with a unique and mysterious architectural style. The 15th-century temple, resembling a stepped pyramid, is dedicated to the Hindu deity Shiva and it symbolises Mount Meru, the cosmic mountain central to Hindu cosmology. Pilgrims have visited Candi Sukuh since its construction, with Maha Shivaratri being a prominent pilgrimage period. The origins of its builders and their strange sculptural style remain a mystery, and it seems to mark a reappearance of the pre-Hindu animism that had existed 1,500 years earlier.

# *Lore Lindu National Park*

## Besoa, Bada, Napu • Sulawesi, Indonesia

The Lore Lindu National Park on the island of Sulawesi in Indonesia has three valleys, Besoa, Bada and Napu. They contain an estimated 400 megalithic granite remains, including differently sized standing statues with human and non-human faces and mysterious chambered containers of immense size called *kalambas*. Some researchers have speculated that these stones were carved more than 5,000 years ago, while others suggest they were created as recently as 1,000 years ago. Equally mysterious are the purpose of the megaliths, the identity of the people that carved them and the source of the stone.

# *Batu Caves Temple*

## Kuala Lumpur • Malaysia

Batu Caves Temple is located approximately 15 km north of Kuala Lumpur, Malaysia, and is famous for its limestone caves and 43-metre-high statue of Muruga. Also known as Kartikeya, Skanda and Subramaniyam, Muruga is the son of Shiva and Parvati (the Hindu goddess of fertility, love and devotion) and the younger brother of the elephant-headed Ganesh. As a Hindu pilgrimage site, Batu Caves has attracted worshippers since the late 19th century. The caves' main temple, Sri Subramaniar Temple, was built in 1891. The most important pilgrimage period is during the annual Thaipusam festival between January and February.

# *Ishibutai Kofun*

## Asuka • Japan

The Ishibutai Kofun, located in Asuka, is Japan's largest known megalithic structure. It is constructed of approximately thirty boulders lining the sides and two enormous roof slabs weighing about 54 and 70 tonnes respectively. Long ago, the entire structure was covered by an earthen mound, which has either eroded or been removed by humans. Contrary to the assumptions of orthodox archaeologists, there is no evidence regarding the age, use or identity of the builders. Furthermore, no burial remains have been excavated within or around the structure. The purpose of this monumental structure remains a complete mystery.

# *Ishi no Hoden*

## Takasago • Japan

Ishi no Hoden (Stone Sanctuary) is a mysterious stone monolith inside the Oshiko Jinja Shinto Shrine in Takasago, Japan. Also called Uki-Ishi (Floating Rock), the strangely shaped rock weighs an estimated 454 tonnes and appears to float above the water's surface. The monolith's origins remain a mystery, with scholars suggesting it was made some time during the Jomon period, dated between 14,000 and 200 BCE. There is no clue as to how the stonemasons carved it due to the lack of historical evidence in the area. No tools or inscriptions/engravings have ever been found near this site.

# *Shinto Shrine of Futami Okitama*

## **Ise • Japan**

Approximately 15 km east of the great Shinto Temple of Ise, and directly on the seacoast of Japan, lies the small Shinto Shrine of Futami Okitama. Two rocks rising from the sea near the shrine known as Meoto Iwa symbolise the Shinto deities Izanagi and Izanami, the divine couple responsible for creating the Japanese islands. The Meoto Iwa, which comprises the 9-metre-high Male Rock and the 4-metre-high Female Rock, connected by an enormous rope, has been a famous symbol of matchmaking as well as a place of worship since ancient times. The site is considered auspicious for married or courting couples.

# *San Agustin Church*

## **Paoay, Luzon • Philippines**

San Agustin Church, situated in Paoay, Luzon, Philippines, is a UNESCO World Heritage Site and a prime example of Filipino Baroque architecture. Established in the 18th century, this historic Roman Catholic church represents a unique fusion of European design and local craftsmanship. The church is prominent in Filipino religious and cultural history and continues to be a vital centre for worship and spirituality. Major Catholic celebrations, such as Easter and Christmas, attract a multitude of visitors.

# *Mount Wollumbin*

## **Australia**

Rising to 1,156 metres on the east coast of Australia, Mount Wollumbin has been considered a sacred place of the Bundjalung Aboriginal people since antiquity. According to Aboriginal lore, Wollumbin is the earthly abode of the Creator, Nguthungulli.

## ABOUT THE AUTHOR

Martin Gray first became fascinated with travel, archaeology, photography and pilgrimage sites while living in India during his early teenage years. Returning to India in his later teens, he began practising Bhakti yoga, the yoga of devotion, which he continued through four decades of pilgrimage to more than 2,000 sacred sites in nearly 170 countries. During these years, he read widely in the fields of mythology, religion and ecology, authored several books and produced the hugely popular World Pilgrimage Guide at sacredsites.com.

# ALSO AVAILABLE

## *Atlas*

Atlas of extreme weather
Atlas of geographical curiosities
Atlas of unusual wines

## *Photo books*

Abandoned America
Abandoned Asylums
Abandoned Australia
Abandoned Belgium
Abandoned churches – Unclamed places of worship
Abandoned cinemas of the world
Abandoned France
Abandoned Italy
Abandoned Japan
Abandoned Lebanon
Abandoned Spain
Abandoned USSR
After the Final Curtain – Vol. 1
After the Final Curtain – Vol. 2
Baikonur – Vestiges of the Soviet Space Programme
Cinemas – A French heritage
Forbidden France
Forbidden Places – Vol. 2
Forbidden Places – Vol. 3
Forgotten Heritage
Oblivion
Unusual hotels
Venice deserted
Venice from the skies

## *'Soul of' guides*

Soul of Amsterdam
Soul of Athens
Soul of Barcelona
Soul of Berlin
Soul of Kyoto
Soul of Lisbon
Soul of Los Angeles
Soul of Marrakesh
Soul of New York
Soul of Rome
Soul of Tokyo
Soul of Venice

## *Secret guides*

Secret Amsterdam
Secret Bali – An unusual guide
Secret Bangkok
Secret Barcelona
Secret Belfast
Secret Berlin
Secret Brighton – An unusual guide
Secret Brooklyn
Secret Brussels
Secret Buenos Aires
Secret Campania
Secret Cape Town
Secret Copenhagen
Secret Corsica
Secret Dolomites
Secret Dublin – An unusual guide
Secret Edinburgh – An unusual guide
Secret Florence
Secret French Riviera
Secret Geneva
Secret Glasgow
Secret Granada
Secret Helsinki
Secret Istanbul
Secret Johannesburg
Secret Lisbon
Secret Liverpool – An unusual guide
Secret London – An unusual guide
Secret London – Unusual bars & restaurants
Secret Los Angeles – An unusual guide
Secret Madrid
Secret Mexico City
Secret Milan
Secret Montreal – An unusual guide
Secret Naples
Secret New Orleans
Secret New York – An unusual guide
Secret New York – Curious activities
Secret New York – Hidden bars & restaurants
Secret Paris
Secret Prague
Secret Provence
Secret Rio
Secret Rome
Secret Seville
Secret Singapore
Secret Sussex – An unusual guide
Secret Tokyo
Secret Tuscany
Secret Venice
Secret Vienna
Secret Washington D.C.
Secret York – An unusual guide

Follow us on Facebook, Instagram and Twitter

Layout: Emmanuelle Willard Toulemonde – Editing: Jana Gough –
Proofreading: Kimberly Bess – Publishing: Clémence Mathé


Registration of copyright: October 2023 – Edition: 01
ISBN: 978-2-36195-684-4
Printed in Slovakia by Polygraf